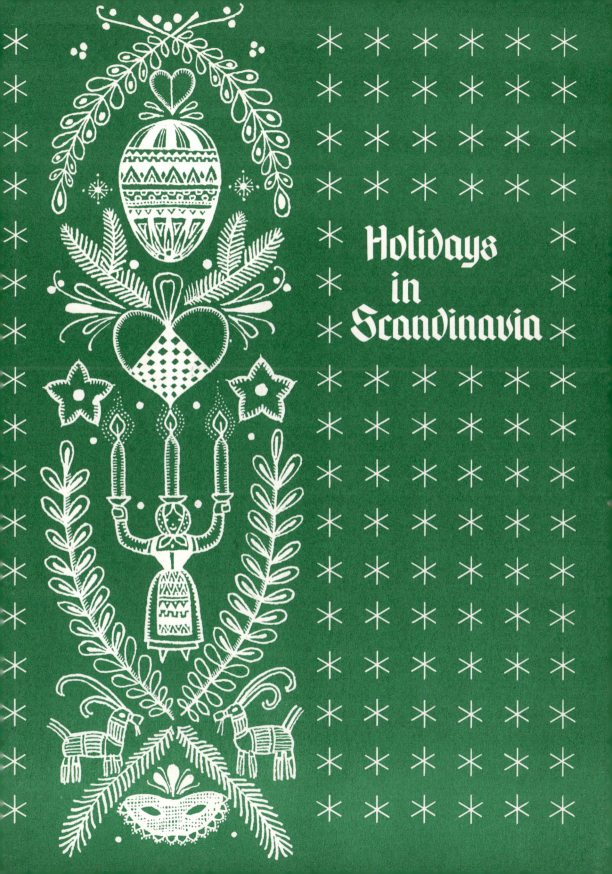

Holidays
in
Scandinavia

Holidays in Scandinavia

By
LEE WYNDHAM
Illustrated by
GORDON LAITE

GARRARD PUBLISHING COMPANY
CHAMPAIGN, ILLINOIS

Library of Congress Cataloging in Publication Data

Wyndham, Lee.
    Holidays in Scandinavia.

    (Around the world holidays)
    SUMMARY: Discusses the origins and celebrations of
the major religious and folk holidays of the Scandinavian countries.

    1. Scandinavia—Description and travel—Juvenile
literature. [1. Holidays—Scandinavia.   2. Scandina-
via—Social life and customs]   I. Laite, Gordon, illus.
II. Title.
DL11.W9   394.2′6948   74–13043
ISBN 0–8116–4955–5

CONTENTS

1. THE VASALOPP:

A Swedish National Ski Festival

Every year, in Sweden, on the first Sunday in March, more than 8,000 skiers take part in the biggest ski race in the world, the Vasalopp. In the first gray light of dawn, they gather on a huge frozen field outside the village of Sälen (Saylen). The men line up ski pole to ski pole, the ends of each racer's skis nearly touching those of the man ahead and the one behind. Some carefully stamp their feet to test the bindings of their lightweight cross-country skis. Some, toward the back, joke about their high starting numbers. Others, going over the route once again in their minds, are tense. All the racers here, whether world champions or only weekend skiers, have spent months in hard physical training for this special event.

The great Vasalopp begins on the border between Norway and Sweden and ends 54 miles away in the old Swedish town of Mora. In between lie hills and long valleys with lakes that must be skirted and deep forests that must be crossed.

It is almost time to start! The seconds tick away. A hush falls over the crowd. Every eye is on the starter, who stands on a high platform where all the racers can see him.

The starting flag snaps down. At once the vast army of skiers surges forward. As the men push off with their poles, there is no sound but the *swish-swish* whisper of their skis and the *clack* of the bindings on their shoes. Soon the runners are far across the snowy field, where 450 years ago a young Swedish hero began a journey that changed the history of his country.

In 1520, when a hated Danish king ruled over Sweden, a young Swedish noble, Gustav Vasa, called on the men of Mora to help him drive out the Danes. The people had often been called to battle against the Danes, and they were tired of fighting and bloodshed. Moreover, it was the Christmas season, a time for peace and home. They refused to listen to the 24-year-old patriot.

With a heavy heart the young man headed for Norway to escape the Danish soldiers who were searching for him. Now the men of Mora changed their minds and decided to fight. The best of their skiers hurried out to overtake Gustav and caught up with him at Sälen. Gustav went back with them, gathered a strong army, and drove the Danes out. Sweden was free, and at 26 Gustav Vasa was elected to be her king.

As Gustavus I, he ruled for almost 40 years—and his descendants held the throne for 250 years more. The Vasa Race, following the route of his return from Sälen to Mora, is held in honor of this brave young king.

Men from all walks of life and ranging in age from 21 to over 60 may enter the marathon race. The rules say only that they must be experienced skiers and their applications must be approved by the Swedish Ski Association. Even so, two or three thousand of them will drop out along the way. Even champion skiers find this a long, tiring race, and to men with less skill or endurance it seems endless.

Swedes consider the Vasa race a test of their manhood, and many men celebrate their 50th birthdays by entering it. Winning the competition is not the goal for most contestants. Only champions in top form can hope to win. Most runners simply hope to finish the 54-mile course. That is glory enough.

There are 40 lanes on the first crowded leg of the course, and the runners streaming over them vie for the front positions. The lanes eventually narrow down to four, and at that point the one hundred or so top skiers out in front begin to battle for the winning spot. "The Vasalopp is so big now—" old-time racers say, "very different from the days when only one or two hundred entered. Then it was a polite race. 'May I pass you, sir?' a runner would call to the man ahead. 'Certainly,' the man would reply and move to one side of the track. Today it is every man for himself. Still, it is a splendid race, is it not?"

The "splendid race" burns up a lot of calories—fast. Runners must eat along the way if they are to have any chance of reaching the finish line. So, energy-rich nourishment is provided at six check-points, spaced about seven miles apart along the course. In front of the rest cabins, food is set out on long tables at which the men may stop briefly without removing their skis. Buckets and pans are kept filled, and rosy-faced women and girls, bundled

up against the cold, serve the men quickly as they glide up. The men may stop for as long as they wish, but the serious competitors drink a mixture of sugar water and lemon juice from paper cups as they move along.

After two or three stops many of the men begin to tire. Only pride keeps some of them going. Even men like Helge Pederson and Sven Olson, both winners of smaller competitions, have trouble toward the end. But they are determined to reach the finish line in the Vasalopp somehow and prove themselves men of spirit. His eyes glazed, Helge pushes one leg before the other. Sven's knees are shaking. The track is terrible. More than a thousand men ahead of them have churned it into rough bumps and deep pits. "Keep going," Helge whispers. Sven nods and smiles wanly for the benefit of a TV camera whirring nearby.

Fifteen or twenty TV cameras and trucks are stationed beside the course at various points. A helicopter, with another camera trained on the racers, hovers overhead. Sports announcers describe the race to the nation. At least half of the eight million people in Sweden watch the dramatic event on television.

All along the course groups of spectators cheer

the runners on. In Mora 30,000 people gather on both sides of the flag-lined Vasagatan, the ski lane that runs through the town. The finish of the run is at the historic statue of the handsome young Gustav Vasa. By late morning the crowd begins to stir restlessly. Soon the winner must glide into sight! Necks are craned. People lean far out to peer up the lane.

Here he comes! With a fine show of strength, he skims down the center of the snowy lane, under the finish-line banner.

"*Heya! Heya! Heya!*" The crowd greets him with the traditional Swedish shout of triumph. Officials surround him. Smiling, he ducks down to let a pretty girl slip a large laurel wreath over his head and onto his shoulders. His picture is snapped by newsmen. People shout congratulations. The winner of the Vasalopp is a national hero. He will get a gold medal to mark his victory and many prizes donated by the sponsors of the race. No cash prize is ever given.

An all-time hero of the race, Jan Stefanson of Sälen, completed the run in 4 hours, 35 minutes, and 3 seconds, one of the shortest times ever recorded. Usually even the strongest skiers take something over five hours. Slower men continue to slog in for hours after the victor. They too are hailed as heroes by welcoming cries of, "Father! Father!" from girls and boys on the sidelines. Or, "Helge! Sven! You have done it!" "*Heya!* Otto!" "Olaf!" "Niles!" No matter when the family hero crosses the finish line, his wife or sweetheart is waiting anxiously with a homemade laurel wreath to drape over *his* shoulders. In her eyes he is as great as the hero in whose honor the race is run. And by completing the course he has proved himself a true son of Sweden.

Those who cross the finish line without going over the winner's time by more than fifty percent are awarded a greatly prized Vasalopp pin. Everyone who finishes before the official closing of the race at 6 P.M. gets a certificate, and his name and running time are listed in the Swedish newspapers.

More than 70,000 men have officially completed the Vasalopp course since the race became a national ski festival in 1922.

2. NORWAY'S HOLMENKOLLEN DAY

The sloping white tower on top of Holmenkollen Hill looks like half a wishbone rising into the sky. Set against a forest of green trees, it can be seen from almost any place in Oslo, the capital of Norway. This is the 184-foot starting point for the world-famous ski-jumping competition held here since 1892, usually on the first Sunday in March. Other ski events go on all during the previous week, but this is "The One" everybody wants to come to see. Some people say, "Holmenkollen is a three-in-one holiday, for it features the national hill, the national holiday, and the national sport."

Norwegians who cannot get there watch the competitions on television. But over 100,000 people usually manage to gather at the hill to see the best "ski birds" from all over the world soar off a platform built on top of a three-story building.

It is cold on the hill, and everyone is bundled into ski pants and jackets and warm wool caps and scarves. Perhaps it is a little warmer in the center of the crowd, for even at the bottom of the rounded landing arena the spectators stand packed shoulder to shoulder. The grandstands, on either side of the "outrun" below the jumping takeoff, are filled with some 8,000 people.

A ripple of excitement runs through the crowd now, and those in the grandstands begin to cheer. "Ah, the royal family has arrived."

Everyone stands at attention as the band plays the royal and the national anthems. The competition can begin!

A trumpet fanfare cuts through the cold, clear air. It means, "The track is clear!" A tiny figure appears at the very top of the starting tower. Faster and faster he hurtles down toward the jump-off platform. Suddenly, off he swoops into the air! His arms are raised, skis held close together. He leans far over them and brings his arms back to his sides, the better to ride the air currents as he tries to stay aloft as long as possible. Down, down he comes, in

a heart-stopping drop, till he hits the track more than 200 feet below the takeoff point. With a quick twist of his body, he stops in a shower of snow.

Again the trumpet cuts through the air. The track is clear for the next "bird," and the next. After each landing a sigh goes up from the huge watching crowd, as if each person there felt the thrill and triumph of the jump. It is a critical audience, for almost everyone in Norway skis. Some even claim that Norwegian children are born with skis on their feet. At any rate, many of them learn to ski almost as soon as they learn to walk. So this is a crowd of "judges," all carefully noting style, speed, and performance. Skis must be lined up just so, the body held precisely in the best ski form. Head, arms— everything is subject to criticism.

When one of the favorites—the ski heroes who have a chance to win the coveted King's Cup— appears at the top of the platform, the cheering begins even before the skier starts from the top of the run. It grows to a roar as he nears the takeoff and shoots out into the air. Foreign skiers receive as great a welcome as the natives. The Holmenkollen spectators are good sportsmen who honor the best skiers, regardless of nationality.

3. A SUN PAGEANT IN NORWAY

Most Scandinavians are sun worshippers, especially after the long months of winter. In Norway wintertime is called *mørketiden* (mur-ka-tee-den) "the murky time." Then the sun never rises high enough to shine into the deep valleys at all and can only be seen from the alps. In the old days, the darkness weighed so heavily on the spirits of the people living in the valleys, that some of them used to climb the mountains on skis just for a glimpse of the sun. Now in many places people glide up to the slopes in a modern cable car, for a few hours of precious light.

In the northernmost parts of Norway, the sun reappears at the end of January or in early February.

This is a signal for celebrating and general good times in many villages. On one day or another at this time, just before noon, teachers suddenly announce that this is *Soldag*, Sun Day. With a whoop, children run to put on their boots and coats and dash outside to play.

In the center of southern Norway, the little town of Rjukan lies in a deep, narrow valley, shut in by towering mountains. People there never see the sun from October 5 to March 12. For them it is indeed a long darkness. They are so overjoyed to see the sun once again that they hold a Sun Pageant in honor of the occasion.

For weeks before the special Sun Day, members of many households are busy putting together fancy costumes. These must fit over layers of warm clothes, for it is cold and the celebrating takes place outdoors.

On Sun Pageant Day the streets of sedate Rjukan are suddenly filled with a strange assortment of people, all streaming toward the town square. Grand ladies and gentlemen of olden times hurry along side by side with clowns and tramps and gypsies— and even small cowboys and Indians, supermen, astronauts, or Viking warriors. Here comes a girl who looks like Snow White, and clinging to her hand is a little Donald Duck. Even many of the old people in the community wear costumes for the big day.

The town square is decorated with glittering ice columns, topped by flaming torches. People crowd into the square, leaving an open space at one end, where a carved chair is set up, like a throne, on a raised wooden platform. A big yellow sun, painted on a dark blue background, seems to rise from behind the empty throne. "That's where the Prince of the Sun will sit," big sister tells the small Donald Duck.

Here he comes! The royal procession enters the square and soon the prince appears. He's dressed in a medieval tunic, short, full breeches, and tights. A cloak is draped over his shoulders, and a soft cap with a dashing feather plume is set upon his head. He is surrounded by a group of young maidens, his *terner*, who are too excited to feel cold in their romantic white gowns. Gloves keep their hands warm, but their tall, cone-shaped hats with floating white veils fluttering at the top offer little protection against the wind. The prince and his attendants are masked, as are most of the spectators.

The procession walks slowly around the square, with the prince nodding graciously to everyone. He moves toward his throne, and his attendants group

themselves around him. The mayor of Rjukan steps up to the prince and places the chain-of-office around his neck. The prince smiles and waves to his subjects. A page hands him a scroll and he reads the order for the day: "Let there be merriment until dawn!"

Loud cheers greet the royal command. Lively music breaks up the crowd into dancing groups of old and young. The prince throws back his royal cloak and dances with many of the lovely masked girls. In between dances everyone watches clowns, acrobats, and magicians performing in the middle of the square. The tempting smells of good things to eat draw people to the booths and shops around the square. But before long singing and folk and modern dancing begin again. The prince returns to his throne when costumes are judged and prizes awarded. On a signal from the Sun Prince, masks are removed, and there is shouting and laughter as the merrymakers recognize each other.

Then, late in the evening, young and old alike gasp at the glory of the fireworks which streak high above the square, toward the dark mountains that surround the town of Rjukan.

The date of the Sun Pageant varies from year to year, but the joy of the occasion is always the same.

4. THE LENTEN SEASON IN SCANDINAVIA

Even in March spring still seems far away in all but the southernmost parts of Scandinavia. Avalanches of snow slide from high-pitched roofs and thud upon the sidewalks. Icicles freeze at night and melt during the day. More snow will fall, perhaps as late as May. And yet the calendar clearly says that the year is moving into spring.

It is almost time for Lent, the period of 40 days traditionally spent in prayer and fasting in preparation for Easter. Sweden, Norway, and Denmark each adopted Lutheranism as a state religion centuries ago. Now most Scandinavians belong to this church and no longer observe the fast days common to the Catholic church during Lent. But the old names of the different days of Lent still remain, and some of the old customs, too. For example, long ago no entertainment was permitted during Lent, and even today Scandinavians make a point of enjoying parties, private masquerades, and formal dinners just before Ash Wednesday when Lent begins, rather than during this period. Some Lenten customs go back to the days when pagan gods were worshiped in Scandinavia.

In Denmark, the Monday before the beginning of Lent is a school holiday. In some parts of the country, the children jump out of their beds at dawn. They arm themselves with "Lenten birches," branches decorated with brightly colored paper flowers. Then they creep into the rooms of their parents and grandparents and waken them by beating the bedclothes with their switches.

"Give buns, give buns, give buns!" they chant, whacking at the covers. Somehow, mysteriously, the "awakened" grown-ups produce the traditional peacemaking buns from beneath the bedcovers. Sometimes candy also is "found" to quiet the noisy switchers. This Danish custom, which is such fun today, grew out of ancient religious rites, brought to Scandinavia by the Vikings. Then people used to switch each other to drive all evil from their bodies. And, in pagan times, they also offered cakes and buns as gifts to the gods and spirits they believed in.

For the Danish children, the early morning buns are not nearly enough to satisfy their appetites for this favorite treat. All during the day they go through the neighborhood trying to collect more. But first they dress up in all sorts of costumes. Some of these are bought in stores. Most are home-made from grown-ups' clothes put together any which way. Even old curtains and sheets will do. Hats are pulled low over the ears. Some of the children wear masks. Others paint or smudge their faces with whatever is handy.

Small groups *knock-knock* on the doors of their neighbors. When the doors swing open, they rattle collection boxes and sing:

> *Buns up, buns down,*
> *Buns for me to chew.*
> *If you don't give me buns to eat*
> *I'll rattle till you do!*

They repeat the chant over and over, jingling the boxes. Most householders don't have that many buns to give, but they cheerfully drop a coin in

each box so the wildly dressed collectors can go to the nearest bakery and buy buns for themselves.

Buns have a place in Swedish Lenten customs, too. Shrove Tuesday, which comes before Ash Wednesday, is known in Sweden as "Fat Tuesday." Besides having a fine dinner, everyone looks forward to the very special dinner treat—a sweet, hot bun called *fettisdagsbulle*. The big bun, four or five inches across, is split and filled with almond paste. The top is sprinkled with powdered sugar and decorated with a thick circle of whipped cream. The bun is served floating on hot milk in large soup plates.

This splendid dessert is so delicious, the people cannot bear to limit it to only one day. Now, if you are invited to a Swedish home for dinner on any Tuesday during Lent, you will no doubt be offered a fettisdagsbulle. But when you taste it, be careful. It is said that an old-time Swedish king could not resist these buns. He ate 20 at one sitting—and died!

During the Lenten season the snow is still thick on the ground, and everyone is heartily tired of winter. To satisfy their longing for spring, some people go out into the woodlands and cut birch twigs to bring home. They tie fluffy chicken feathers, dyed in brilliant reds, yellows, purples, oranges, and greens, to the branches and put the twigs into vases filled with water.

When the vases are set in the living room windows, the warmth of the houses and the increasing spring sunshine soon force the twigs to put out tender green leaves. These bright bouquets "bloom" on thousands of windowsills, and suddenly it seems that spring has come.

Easter Witches

In pagan times the people of Scandinavia believed that several times each year witches flew over the land to meet the demons who were their masters. Such meetings were called Witches' Sabbaths. At each one the creatures heard the demons' suggestions for evil deeds to keep them busy until the next Witches' Sabbath. Even long after Scandinavians became Christians the belief persisted, and the Thursday before Easter, *Skartorsdag*, was thought to be a day when witches flew to their secret meeting place.

The dark superstitions of ancient days are gone, but today little Swedish girls take special delight in playing "Easter Hags." Early in the afternoon on the Saturday before Easter, the day when the witches flew back from the meeting to their homes, the girls begin to get ready. Each dresses up in some old skirt of mother's, tucks in a baggy blouse, and ties a bright kerchief round her head. A besom broom, made of a bundle of twigs tied together, or an ordinary old one is fine to "ride." A shiny copper kettle is a must. And then with an old lady shawl thrown around her shoulders and some soot smeared on her face, the "hag" is ready to terrify the neighborhood.

Little Easter witches ring doorbell after doorbell and shake their copper kettles. To avoid having a wicked spell cast over them, the properly frightened neighbors toss coins or candies into the kettles. The pleased witches curtsy and scamper off, giggling, to the next doorway. Before long their kettles are full, and they hurry home to help dye eggs.

Easter Eggs

On this Saturday before Easter pots and bowls of hardboiled eggs stand on most kitchen tables in Sweden. Jars and glasses filled with brilliant dyes are ready for the dipping, and the children can hardly wait to begin. It's a family party. Even the baby's chubby hand is guided through the dipping of an egg.

The main meal of the day consists chiefly of hardboiled eggs. The members of some families compete to see who can eat the greatest number. No matter how many are eaten, in all three Scandinavian countries mothers set aside enough for the egg hunts which are a part of Easter Sunday.

Once the children are safely in bed, parents tiptoe through the house and garden finding places to hide the brightly painted eggs. They tuck some eggs among the branches of the shrubbery, and hide others cunningly in places around the house —in flowerpots and doll beds and behind the tall carved clock that came from great-grandfather's farm.

Danish parents hide the eggs in the gardens and homes in "rabbits' nests," which they make of small round mounds of paper straw. Or they hide eggs in baskets tucked into unlikely places, or cluster them in little heaps on a napkin. Next morning shrieks of delight greet each find, for these Danish "rabbits" leave chocolate and decorated sugar eggs as well as dyed hens' eggs for the lucky hunters.

In Norway, weeks before Easter, children beg their mothers to make scrambled eggs, cakes and puddings, and anything else they can think of that uses lots of eggs. What they're really after are the eggshells, and their mothers know it. Whenever a Norwegian mother is ready to use eggs in a recipe, she calls the children into the kitchen. Instead of cracking the eggs, she allows the young people to make a small hole in both ends of each egg and carefully blow out the contents into the cooking bowl.

The empty shells are hoarded until a few days before Easter when they are dyed or hand-painted and decorated with paste-on designs.

Some children draw a string or ribbon through the egg holes and hang the beautiful eggs for display in a window, on a light fixture, or on some house plant.

Easter Day in Scandinavia

In Norway, Lent ends with a glorious holiday, from Thursday through Monday, and almost everyone is determined to get out of the towns and cities for the five days. Whole families, groups of friends of all ages, clubs, and couples, all loaded with skates and skis and weekend gear, hurry to railroad and bus stations. Soon the trains and buses bristle with skis set upright into special racks. Those who have cars hurry to finish loading them. Long skis, fastened into brackets on top of tiny autos, make the cars look like beetles turned upside down. Here a family is refastening a big toboggan that has slid to one side; there children are shouting to a sister to *hurry* and get whatever it is she has forgotten in the house. In a few hours the streets are almost deserted, and those few people who cannot leave look longingly toward the snow-clad mountains.

The lucky ones going away will be outdoors, enjoying the sun and air as long as the daylight lasts. Then, some will go inside to dance or listen to concerts. Others will continue to skate or to ski and toboggan on the floodlighted slopes.

Religious observance of Easter is not forgotten. Many celebrate the holiday with an early morning church service before leaving town. But more and more people now combine the religious traditions with their sports activities. Scandinavians are sometimes called "blue domers" because they like to hold services under the blue dome of the sky instead of in a closed building. Some of the mountain centers have sunrise services outdoors on Easter morning. Near Oslo there are open-air chapels along the ski trails for the worshipers who spend their Sundays regularly in the rolling countryside.

Here they arrive on skis in a clearing surrounded by a forest of evergreens. Skis and poles are quickly stacked in racks, and the people file to the simple wooden benches set in the clearing. Before them is a roughhewn wooden altar topped by a plain wooden cross. They enjoy a few moments of meditation in these peaceful surroundings before the minister, dressed in traditional robes, steps forward to lead the morning prayers. Hymns rise to the blue sky on the cold, crisp air, and then skis are put on once more and the skiers are off and away. Very likely the minister takes off his robes, puts on his skis, and he, too, is off for his ski holiday.

In Sweden the Easter holiday lasts only four days, Friday through Monday. There, too, people board special excursion trains and rush off by the thousands into the mountains. Those who stay at home spend Easter Monday visiting friends and relatives and sipping tall glasses of the traditional *äggtoddy*, a delicious mixture of egg yolk, sugar, sherry, and boiling water.

5. SWEDEN'S WALPURGIS EVE

Huge crowds gather in the pale dusk on the hillsides of Sweden's favorite island park, Skansen, on the outskirts of Stockholm. Even though it is the Eve of May First, people are bundled up warmly, for there is a fresh breeze from the sea. Behind them twinkle the lights of Stockholm, but tonight few look down toward the city. Everyone is much more interested in what is about to happen on Reindeer Mountain, the hilltop rising directly above them.

As the night deepens, a growing feeling of excitement grips the crowd. It cannot be much longer! Then suddenly there is a blaze of light on the hilltop and a crackling roar as flames from a tremendous log and tar-barrel fire leap into the night sky. All eyes are fixed upon the fire, now visible for miles around the island. "Is it a magic fire?" a small child's voice pipes up in the crowd.

In the gathering darkness, made deeper by the scarlet tongues of flame, it is easy to believe, as people did long ago, that such fires *are* magic. Surely they will frighten away any witches and trolls who might be about and rid the country of their evil influence until the spring crops have been sown.

The stirring ceremony of Walpurgis Eve has survived from Viking days, when the warriors held annual feasts in honor of the returning sun and warmth. They lit huge roaring bonfires on the mountaintops and banged their sword hilts against their tough leather shields. The thud against the wood and leather echoed like thunder. The clang of metal rang out into the night. And in the flickering light of the red flames, the bearded warriors in their rough tunics and furs must have looked especially fierce. Surely this frightening scene sent the demons of darkness and gloom scuttling elsewhere, as it was meant to do.

When the Scandinavians were converted to Christianity, they did not easily forget their old fears and would not give up their pagan rituals. The church then pointed out that this particular spring rite fell on one of the feast days of Saint Walpurga. Walpurga was a good, wise, and learned lady who had lived in the eighth century. After her death she was honored as a saint, and it was believed that she worked many miracles. So these new Christians, though they held to their old customs, also began to pray to her for protection from witches and spirits of darkness, especially on her feast day. Gradually the Eve of May First came to be known by her name: Walpurgis Eve.

Today Walpurgis Eve is celebrated throughout the whole of Sweden as a spring festival. The kindling of bonfires on the hills and mountains is a welcome to the lengthening days, not a means of frightening away the witches and demons. Even though snowflakes may fall hissing into the flames, the Swedes raise their voices in spring songs. "A, hur härlight majsol ler," they sing. "O, how beautifully the May sun smiles."

In smaller towns and villages young people sometimes dance around the bonfires in a ring. Old people study the flames to see if they blow to the north or south. If to the north, spring will be late, and cold. If to the south, they smile. Spring will be early and mild.

The Spring Capping at Uppsala

By midafternoon on April 30, in the ancient Swedish city of Uppsala, thousands of students stand in front of the university library on the hill. Each carries hidden in a pocket a "student cap" made of white velvet, with a shiny black visor.

These are precious caps, earned through years of hard study in a *gymnasium*, or secondary school. Only gymnasium graduates have the right to wear them. The custom began in the nineteenth century and is now a tradition. Swedish men and women keep their student caps all their lives and wear them for all sorts of special occasions.

The university students have not worn their white caps since cold weather set in. On Walpurgis Eve, those at Uppsala prepare to put them on for the first time that year, as part of their student spring festival. Now, crowded outside the library, they move restlessly, but their eyes never leave a university official standing on a balcony. The man has a watch in his hand. He is counting the seconds. On the stroke of three o'clock, he whips out his white cap and waves it high overhead.

Instantly the students pull out their caps and, with a tremendous shout, wave them high in the air. The caps flutter like a flock of white birds. On signal, there is silence. A speaker appears on the balcony.

He speaks of what has been accomplished by Uppsala students in the past, of what can be accomplished in the future. But he does not talk for long. He is wise! "Let us now join in a fourfold cheer for our Nordic spring," says he. "Long may she live!"

"*Hurra! Hurra! Hurra! Hurra!*" Four cheers ring out—and then one more for good measure.

Hurriedly the students pull their caps on tight and wheel about to face the broad avenue that leads downhill into the ancient town square. They form lines, link arms, and start a headlong rush downward, shouting, laughing, shrieking. Nothing and no one had better stand in the way. It is an awesome sight! The townspeople are used to it and stand safely out of the way at upper-story windows to watch the goings on.

When the first lines reach the square, they turn about and charge back up the hill. With a roar they crash into the students still running down to the square. A "battle" begins. Students push and pull and shove one another. Each group tries to force the other out of the way, but it's all in fun. Everybody is laughing, and nobody wins or loses in this spring "battle," which goes on for the rest of the afternoon.

Twilight brings a change of mood. The students, now quiet and solemn, take up lighted torches and march in silence toward the library. Twenty thousand strong, they form a great chain of flickering lights winding up the dark hillside.

On the crest of the hill stands a huge red castle. (It was begun by Gustav Vasa around 1550 and is now the residence of the governor of the province of Uppland.) At the foot of the round north tower, there is a tall wooden belfry. Here hangs the ancient "Queen Gunilla Bell," which is rung every day at six in the morning and at nine o'clock at night.

As the last of the students reach the high castle hill, the bell strikes nine. Now the men's university choir comes marching up from the town.

The thousands of white-capped students stand

silent, while in the distance fireworks smack and bang and hiss off into the night sky, and the flames of Walpurgis Eve bonfires in countless villages brighten the flatlands below. The choir assembles, and the conductor's wand comes down. Strong young men's voices break into the traditional student songs. Most of these songs praise the returning spring. And always there is the special song: "O, sing of the student's happy days!"

Later, after the student association president makes his speech of welcome to spring, there is more cheering for king and country. Then the young people stream away to have supper at restaurants and homes, or at one of the thirteen student clubs, called "nations."

All the nations and restaurants and homes resound with the noise of happy celebration. No one thinks of going to bed. Any old-time witches who happen to fly past Uppsala on this Walpurgis Eve–Student Spring Festival Night, must surely fly higher—and faster—for fear of what might happen if the celebrating students ever got hold of them!

6. CONSTITUTION DAY IN NORWAY

On May 17, every schoolboy and girl in Norway, and most of the grown-ups, must be out of bed at the crack of dawn. There is no need to set an alarm clock. In most towns and villages a tremendous *boom* from a cannon, or a *bang* from a gun salutes the day. For this is Norway's greatest national holiday, the day on which her constitution was signed in 1814. The celebrating and the parades start early.

The biggest parade is in Oslo, the capital city. Always in the lead are the school children. While some 30,000 children assemble for the three-hour march, crowds of spectators stream toward the flag-draped streets. They carry box lunches and flags, small red banners with blue and white crosses. Many wear bunches of ribbons or rosettes in the national colors. Most of the people try to find a place along the broad main avenue that leads to the palace grounds, but soon all the parade streets as well as the palace grounds are packed. Space in front of the palace is reserved for children from the city hospitals. The air is filled with the scent of lilacs. Everybody is happy, laughing and talking.

A roll of drums is heard. The spirited tootling of the first brass band grows louder. Here they come! Line upon line of marchers swings into view. People on the sidelines wave their small flags wildly.

As the girls and boys march past the front of the royal palace, they look upward, smile, and wave their flags. On a balcony above the marchers, the king and the royal family smile back warmly at the children. The men of the family raise their hats in salute, the ladies bow and wave. Under the balcony the long line seems endless. The musicians are brilliant in their band uniforms of blue, green, or red. The girls and boys look neat and clean in their best clothes, or fresh and colorful in richly embroidered regional costumes.

Next in line are the students who will graduate

in June from the gymnasia, senior high schools. They wear scarlet caps with long blue tassels and carry jaunty bamboo canes. As they pass the royal family, the students cheer and twirl their bright caps up in the air on the ends of the canes. The young people are happy and proud, and the royal family beams down upon them.

Trade unions and other organizations follow the students. Often they have gaily decorated cars and floats as part of their procession.

Though this parade is the largest, every town and village has a procession of some kind, with bands playing and flags waving. Wherever the celebration is held, many of the marchers are certain to be dressed in their special regional costumes.

Each district or valley has its own style of *bunad*, or embroidered costume. If a family moves, the bunad goes with it and is worn proudly wherever they settle. Anyone who knows the various patterns used can tell which valley a girl comes from by the type of costume she wears. The men and boys in Norway do not usually wear regional dress, unless they are going to perform in a folk festival, a dance, or a music group.

After the big Constitution Day parades, each

neighborhood has a celebration of its own in the afternoon. Children who are too little to join in the long school parades march near their homes. They all wave the red, white, and blue flags and very seriously sing the national anthem of Norway:

> *Norway, thine is our devotion*
> *Land of hearth and home,*
> *Rising storm-scarr'd o'er the ocean,*
> *Where the breakers foam.*

Grown-ups bring up the rear of the children's parade. Mothers push baby carriages, and fathers carry toddlers on their shoulders. Every one heads for a park or field to listen to patriotic speeches. The people sing patriotic songs and shout cheers for king and country and flag. No one forgets the meaning of this national day.

Afterward they have a splendid picnic, followed by games, jumping contests, and fun races, like "egg-on-a-spoon."

In the evening there is usually a feast in the village hall. Then there's music and folk dancing. As the night goes on, the excitement grows. The dances get faster and faster, the laughter merrier, for everyone must be happy and gay on May seventeenth. And in Norway, everyone is!

7. THE BIRTHDAY
OF THE DANISH FLAG

Not only do the Danes say that theirs is the oldest kingdom in the world, they also claim to have the oldest national flag, the *Dannebrog*. This flag was "born" more than 750 years ago, and its birthday is celebrated on June fifteenth.

Every Danish child is taught the legend of the flag's origin. And, at one time or another, most of them take part in the pageants that tell about it.

In mid-June some school, club, sports organization, or local Boy Scout troop is sure to put on a pageant. Dressed in cleverly made thirteenth century soldiers' costumes, the young people fight fiercely in make-believe battle. Silver-painted wooden swords gleam and clatter. The boys cheer as one group seems to push the other back. Then the losing side appears to gain. Back and forth the "battle" goes.

The young people are acting out the legend of the Dannebrog and King Valdemar. According to this legend, in the year 1219 the Danish king, Valdemar, led an expedition against the pagan Estonians. His goal was to conquer them and make them Christians.

During the night of June fifteenth, the Estonians made a surprise attack on the Danish camp and soon were winning the battle. On a nearby hill, the old Danish archbishop stretched his arms toward heaven and prayed to God for help. While he held his arms up, the Danes pushed back the enemy. But when the old man lowered his arms from weariness, the Estonians gained ground. Suddenly there was a great peal of thunder, and a red banner with a white cross floated down from the sky. As it fell into the archbishop's arms, a voice from the clouds said: "When you raise this banner against your enemies, they will yield before you."

The archbishop immediately sent a messenger with the banner to King Valdemar on the battlefield. The king held the banner high. And this miraculous sign from heaven gave the Danes fresh courage. They fell upon the Estonians and won.

The Danes love their national emblem and fly it on all special occasions, or simply because it's a "lovely day." Visitors in Denmark are always astonished by the numbers of flagstaffs they see.

The flag is hoisted in villages by friends and neighbors of people celebrating weddings and round-figure birthdays. When the twins, Knud and Karen Holm were ten, the flags waved up and down their street in Odense. And when Kaj Hansen, the boat builder in a seaport town on the Kattegat Strait, celebrated his sixtieth birthday, not only did all the flags in town fly, but on all the boats in the harbor, flags were raised in his honor.

Of course every official "flag holiday," such as the Queen's Birthday, is faithfully observed. On festival days the flag decorates the city streets and is displayed in store windows. But on June fifteenth everywhere you turn there's the Dannebrog, snapping in the breeze! For June fifteenth is Flag Day, when the Danes celebrate the miraculous appearance of their beloved Dannebrog. Even though many flags are flown daily, on this day thousands of red and white banners are raised to the sky.

51

8. MIDSUMMER IN THE
LAND OF THE MIDNIGHT SUN

By the middle of June, in Scandinavia, there is but a thin veil of twilight between one day and the next. For weeks now, the sun has risen earlier and earlier and set later and later. This land, which only a few months ago lay in darkness, is now bathed in sunshine. In the southern part of Sweden, the sun only *begins* to set at 10 P.M., and it is up again at 2 A.M.! In Oslo, Norway, there are more than 20 hours of light each day. And in Denmark the Danes happily say, "The season of bright nights is upon us." For a few wonderful weeks of summer they have almost 18 hours of light each day to make up for their long dark winter.

52

Below the Arctic Circle, the sun cannot be seen at midnight. But above it, the great golden disk shines brightly 24 hours a day for six long weeks. And at Norway's North Cape, the northernmost point of Europe, the sun does not set from mid-May to the end of July—a ten- or eleven-week "day"!

In all of Scandinavia daylight round the clock makes people feel lighthearted, even a bit light-headed. No one seems to need much sleep. There's a strange feeling in the air, as if something wonderful were about to happen. And of course it does, with the celebration of Midsummer Eve. Since pagan days, this time of magical sunlight has been celebrated, and today it is the most important holiday of the year, except for Christmas.

Pagan celebrations of the past probably took place on the night of June 21, the longest day of the year. The pagans worshiped the sun and on this day built huge bonfires in its honor. After the Christian faith was adopted in Scandinavia, the Church chose to celebrate Midsummer on June 24, along with the birthday of *Sankt Hans*, or Saint John. June 23 became known as Saint John's Eve, or *Jonsok* in Norway and *Sankt Hans Aften* in Denmark. On that night in both of these countries, enormous bonfires send long tongues of flame into the sky, just as in the old, old times. But today's fires merely symbolize the joy and lightheartedness of the season.

Norway's Jonsok

As the brightest light of day begins to fade on Saint John's Eve, Norway's shores, mountains, and valleys glow with hundreds of fires. Fireworks hiss and zoom off into the deepening twilight blue of the sky. They burst and fall back in glittering showers. The air is fresh and clear, and everyone feels how wonderful it is to be alive.

Norwegians who live near the fiords head for the water's edge. There motor launches, decorated with green boughs and flowers, wait at piers to take passengers out onto the deep sea inlets. As the boats chug up and down the fiords, the passengers get the best possible view of the Saint John's fires on the mountains. People in every village, resort, and vacation cottage celebrate this special eve with bonfires and fireworks.

On land, near the blazing fires, groups in folk costumes dance to the old tunes played on fiddles and accordions. As one musician "plays himself out" and steps back, another takes his place. There is no break in the music the whole night through. The dancers whirl about and leap high into the air; the girls are swung dizzyingly by their partners. Faster, faster they go until, panting for breath, they run off to fling themselves on the grass, and another group takes their place.

Music and dancing are only part of the all-night fun. Farther from the fires laughing boys and girls may lurch about in a three-legged race. When they tire of that, they scramble into sacks and hop toward their goal like huge rabbits.

Or a crowd may gather around the base of a tall pole. There's a valuable prize at the top for the one who can get to it. "Maybe a soccer ball?" Alfred guesses. "I could use a new knapsack," says Axel. "And I a fishing pole," adds Harald.

"Here I go!" shouts Alfred, but he doesn't go far. The pole has been greased, and it is very slippery! Axel fares no better. Harald manages to shinny halfway to the top, then slides back, catches hold —somehow—and just manages to reach the top. He makes a wild grab, gets hold of the prize, and whizzes down, tumbling to the ground. "Hey! What do you know! It *is* a fishing rod," he calls out, as

his friends pull him to his feet and thump him on the back.

In the country, men and boys still follow the old custom of taking a running jump over the bonfires, for, "As high as you jump over Saint John's fires, so high will the grain grow in the coming year," they say. The jumping is usually done at the close of the celebration, when the flames are low over the embers.

Denmark's Sankt Hans Aften

In Denmark an effigy, a crude figure, of a witch is sometimes set on top of a brushwood fire. This is a leftover custom from the old days of superstition and has nothing to do with Sankt Hans. But the witch does stand for the spirit of evil and darkness that everyone wants to be rid of. She looks terribly real as she bursts into flame, and the wide-eyed Danish children, watching the fire, shriek when her glowing fragments fly in all directions.

Sweden's Midsommar

"The day that never ends!" That is what the Swedish people often call Midsummer Eve. They celebrate *Midsommar* on the nearest Saturday to June 24, so that most of them won't have to worry about going to work the next day. The celebrating starts on Friday, Midsummer Eve, and goes on right through Sunday. Every home and public building is decorated with fresh green birch boughs and flowers. Apartment houses, shop doors, porches, balconies, private automobiles, buses, taxis, ships, and small pleasure boats—all wear these signs of the festival of summer.

People flock to the province of Dalarna for the festival weekend. Here in the heart of Sweden, much of the country's history was made. (It was here that Gustav Vasa raised his army to fight the invading Danes.) Among the misty blue, tree-covered mountains, the lakes, and the green valleys lie tiny villages where some of Sweden's oldest wooden cottages are preserved as historic relics and museums. The people of Dalarna are especially determined to keep traditions and customs of the past.

The symbol of the holiday is the Midsummer Pole, the *majstång* (maystong). *Stång* means pole, and *maj* comes from an old Swedish verb which means "to decorate with flowers and leaves."

A few days before the holiday, the men go into the forest to choose a pine or spruce for the majstång. Ah! Here is the perfect tree. It is tall and straight and slender as a ship's mast. *Thock! Thock!* Axes fly as two of the young men cut the tree down. A team of six strips it of its branches; another team peels off the bark. Several men lift the pole to their shoulders, and singing lustily, "We roam o'er the hills drenched with dew, fa-la-la," the whole troop marches it back to the open field where it will be set up. They lay the pole down across supports so it is well off the ground and ready for decorating.

On the afternoon before Midsummer Eve, the girls of the village go into the countryside to gather basketfuls of wild flowers. At the same time, young men and boys cut hundreds of birch branches and heap them outside a large barn near the field.

Next morning, right after breakfast, young and old gather at the spacious barn which is used for dances and all sorts of village affairs. The wide doors are thrown open, and the boys struggle in with loads of birch branches piled so high they can't see over the top. They stagger and bump into the girls with the flower baskets and the women bringing in coils of wire, decorations, rope, and string. There is a hustle-bustle of confused directions, good-natured scolding, and much laughter before everyone settles down to work.

Baskets of flowers are passed down the long tables set upon trestles. Heaps of birch are laid beside the benches where the women and girls begin to make wreaths. Even bigger heaps are used to make long green garlands. Groups of women and girls twine the soft branches around ropes the men have strung along the walls within comfortable arms' reach. Before long, stepladders are set up, and the yards and yards of garlands are fastened high on the walls to decorate the barn with great loops of green. Tucking flowers in among the tender green leaves, nimble fingers fly to finish one last special garland.

"Now we take it out!" someone shouts.

And, singing, "In summer the sun shines so clearly," or some other old song, everyone helps carry the long garland and other decorations to the Midsummer Pole. The women twine the leafy garland round and round the pole and hang wreaths of greens and flowers from a crossbar set near the top. Someone fastens the blue and yellow

Swedish flag at the very top. Someone else ties a brightly painted wooden rooster, just below the flag. The pole is properly decked out now, and it's nearly eleven o'clock!

"Hurry! We must dress!" several voices call out, and everybody rushes away to put on the gay costumes traditional in that particular church district, or parish. Many of these garments are family treasures, handed down from parent to child, and kept for special occasions.

Soon it is time to raise the pole and ease it into the deep hole which has been dug for it. The raising of the majstång is a traditional rite in which every man, woman, and child likes to take a hand. So everyone flocks back to the village green. The men line up on both sides of the pole. Fourteen are needed to raise this 36-foot majstång! The men use ropes and thin, sturdy, crossed sticks (tied securely together near the top) to pull and push the Midsummer Pole into place. Every eye is fixed upon the operation. Fiddlers from the village stand ready, their bows poised over their instruments.

The man in charge of the activities calls a signal. "*Ett å två å tre!* (One and two and three!)"

With a heave and a push, up goes the pole, and

up goes a tremendous cheer: *"Hurra! Hurra! Hurra!"* The men strain to hold the majstång steady as it sways against the background of blue sky. Now they wedge it firmly into the hole. The fiddlers' bows come down! The summer air is filled with the lilting tune of an old "round" dance.

The smallest children join hands and form a circle close to the Midsummer Pole. Circle upon circle of children and grown-ups forms around them to dance to the old tunes. Later young men and women dance in couples around the majstång. Smiling crowds gather to watch as the girls are whirled round their partners, skirts swirling and feet so light and quick in the intricate steps that must be done just so.

Other folk dances follow—the Windmill Dance, the Three Karls Polka, the Ox Dance. Oh, but it is fun to dance and fun to watch and clap.

All Sweden echoes with the happy sounds of Midsommar celebrations. Everywhere whole families take part. And when the youngest children have been put to bed, the dancing continues in the fields, or in outdoor pavilions, or perhaps in a large village barn, or out on a pier near a lake. In Rättvik (Ret-veek), on Lake Siljan, at least one

person, carried away by the excitement of the day, is sure to tumble into the water.

As this "day that never ends" lengthens, young people whirl about to the strains of modern music, too. While they dance, the sun barely dips below the rim of hills, then rises again, brilliantly. And, wherever the celebration is held, it goes on and on, for no one seems to get tired on this magical Midsummer Day.

9. THE CHRISTMAS SEASON
IN SCANDINAVIA

The longest holiday celebration in all Scandinavia is Christmas. As this season approaches, the days grow very short. Only a few hours of gray light lie between the darkness of morning and the darkness of evening. Electric lights are on all the time, inside the houses and out on the streets. They somehow lose their cheerfulness after a while, and everyone in the southern regions begins to long for snow to brighten the dreary landscape. But even the snow of the north is not much help when the bleak Scandinavian winter sets in in earnest.

Advent

And then, when feelings are at lowest ebb, comes
Advent. This month-long period of spiritual preparation for Christmas is also a busy time of cooking,
cleaning, and gift-making. All this activity begins
on the First Sunday in Advent, when Swedish
mothers take out a traditional candle holder. Usually the holder is an oblong of brass, made to hold
four candles in a row. The candles are always
white and decorated at the base with small evergreens, tiny fir cones, and red berries.

Mother lights one candle on Advent Sunday and
allows it to burn down an inch or so. On the
Second Sunday she lights both the first and the
second candle and lets them burn down an inch.
On the Third Sunday three are lit, and on the
Fourth Sunday, all four. By now they look like
small organ pipes, ready to make Christmas music.

Early in the Advent season Christmas lights begin to appear. Many families hang a large Advent
Star in their windows, and its golden glow is a
welcome beacon in the darkness. Whole rows of
houses in the towns and cities sparkle with decorations in crystal clear lights. Parks, town squares,
shopping centers—all begin to shine. Strings of

clear lights, with large hanging golden stars, are looped over the streets in towns and cities. In Stockholm, Scandinavian boats in the harbor always have small, lighted fir trees fixed to their masts. And tiny trees with diamond-bright lights outline the many city bridges.

All over Sweden Christmas lights are glowing weeks before the holiday season officially begins with Saint Lucia's Day on December thirteenth. And they will continue to brighten the dark days until Saint Knut's Day, on January thirteenth, when the season officially ends.

Lucia's Day

Before Lucia's Day, or *Luciadagen*, everything on the farms and in the homes must be put in order. Housewives clean their houses from top to bottom. Floors are scrubbed, windows washed. Every piece of furniture is waxed and polished, and fresh curtains are hung. Silver, copper, pewter—whatever the family owns—is polished to its brightest sheen. Everything must reflect and welcome the Queen of Light, Saint Lucia.

Just how Lucia became an honored saint in Sweden is a mystery, for she was born in Italy, in the third century. Some believe that her story was brought to Sweden by Viking traders who had become Christians. Lucia lived in the days when Christians were cruelly treated by the pagan Roman government. And yet, while still a young girl, Lucia became a Christian and gave her wealth to the poor. According to legend, she suffered a martyr's death under Emperor Diocletian, on December thirteenth, A.D. 304. Later she was declared a saint by the church and given the name of Saint Lucia.

Her name means "light." And because she died at the turning point of the year, when the nights begin to get shorter and the day's light lasts longer and longer, she became a symbol of light to the sun-starved people of the North. They imagined Lucia as a shining figure crowned by a radiant halo.

At one time, during the Middle Ages, there was a terrible famine in the province of Värmland. When the suffering of the people was almost unbearable, it is said, a large white vessel loaded with food and clothing appeared on Lake Vänern. At the helm stood a beautiful maiden in a gleaming white robe, her head encircled by a crown of radiant beams. As soon as the ship was unloaded, it vanished. The grateful people believe that the maiden who had come to save them was Saint Lucia. This good saint is still loved and honored in Sweden today.

It is not yet dawn on Saint Lucia's Day when Swedish mothers awaken their children. Together they will prepare "bread for hunger and candles to light the darkness" which are part of the Lucia Day ceremony. First come the Lucia costumes. The oldest daughter, dressed in a long robe of white, tied with a crimson sash, represents the saint. On her head she wears a metal crown, the base of which is covered with the green leaves of the lingonberry, the mountain cranberry. Sometimes tiny-leaved ilex, or some other evergreen leaf is used. Five, seven, or even nine white candles are set into Lucia's crown.

While Lucia adjusts her crown to be sure it cannot slip, mother turns to the younger girls. All of them, down to the smallest toddler who can be trusted to hold a candle wrapped in a damp handkerchief, must also be dressed in white. Then circlets of silver tinsel, like glittering halos, are placed upon their heads. The boys, who are called *Starngossar*, or Star Boys, slip into white robes also and put on tall cone-shaped hats made of silver paper, decorated with cutouts of stars.

The grown-up members of the family—father, aunts, uncles, grandparents—are supposed to sleep through all the excitement of these preparations. They must remain deaf to the whisperings, titterings, and hushing sounds. They cannot hear the clinks of dishes set on trays as the traditional breakfast is prepared. They must sleep so soundly that the smell of coffee and the fragrance of warm Lucia buns and ginger cookies does not waken them.

When all is ready, the procession forms. Mama checks the damp handkerchief placed for safety on top of Lucia's hair and lights the candles. The crown is heavy and Lucia must be careful of the flickering flames. And there's the full tray to manage. Lucia closes her eyes and prays. "Please let everything go smoothly. Don't let me trip and fall. And please don't let wax drip into my hair. It is so difficult to get out."

Mama checks the candles of the other children and lights them. Lucia takes up her tray, and walking carefully and slowly, leads the troop to father's door.

She listens. There is no sound in the room. He must be asleep. Behind her there is a shuffling of feet, a clearing of throats. Softly mama sounds the pitch and the children begin the traditional song:

Santa Lucia, thy light is glowing
Through darkest winter night, comfort bestowing.
Dreams float on wings tonight,
Comes then the morning light,
Santa Lucia, Santa Lucia.

Verse after verse they sing. The tune is an old Italian air which also somehow found its way to Sweden.

Before all the verses are finished, one of the Star Boys opens the bedroom door. He swings it wide, and Lucia steps into the room.

Father awakens at the proper moment. He blinks at the glory of the radiant Lucia and her small followers. He sits up and delightedly accepts coffee and the special saffron *Lusse* or *Lussekatter* (Lucia Cats), buns shaped like a curly fat X with a currant at each of the four curled-over corners. *Pepparkakor*, ginger cookies shaped into hearts and stars, are also offered to him, while the children continue to sing. Then the procession moves to the

bedsides of other members of the family and greets them in the same way.

The grandparents and aunts think the children look like angels. Their eyes mist with loving tears. The uncles agree the children look beautiful, but couldn't they have come an hour or two later? Hot coffee restores their humor somewhat. With the ceremony over, the grown-ups blow out the candles, and the youngsters settle on the beds to nibble the goodies and drink the hot cocoa mother now brings in.

This is the family celebration. But so lovely a ceremony could not be kept at home forever. In recent years the Lucia tradition has developed into a community festival observed in schools, offices, and hotels. Specially chosen Lucias and their attendants appear in hospitals to cheer the old and ailing. The biggest public celebration is in Stockholm, where hundreds of girls compete for the honor of being the "Stockholm Lucia."

Christmas Preparations

Nothing seems so busy or smells so delicious as a Swedish kitchen between Lucia's Day and *Julafton*, Christmas Eve. The women and girls of the family hurry and scurry about all day and half the evening preparing the special holiday foods. There is endless weighing and measuring of ingredients, stirring, beating, whipping, kneading, pouring batter, rolling out dough. Pans and cookie sheets slide in and out of the ovens. The girls and little boys, eager to cut their share of cookie dough and to decorate the cookies, crowd around the mothers and aunts and grandmothers. And of course, all those pans and spoons must be licked!

When the cupboard shelves are loaded with tin boxes full of different kinds of cookies, the families turn their attention to the decorations which every Swedish home must have. Older people make lacy paper cutouts to mount on the walls, while the younger children put together yards and yards of paper chains.

Then one night father and big brother bring out the tree ornaments from the attic. Boxes are opened, and everything is lovingly examined by the whole family. Here are the small *Julbockar*, the Yule goats, and the little *Julgrisar*, the Yule pigs, to hang on the tree. These traditional animals are cleverly made of tied, twisted, bent, and braided straw.

Here is the big Julbock with long braided straw horns. He is as tall as the five-year-old in the family and will stand under the tree. Father carefully removes the paper wrappings from the big straw goat. "My father's father made this Julbock for our first Christmas, after your mama and I were married," he tells the children.

The use of straw animals is a tradition, left over from pagan Norse celebrations. In the old mythology, these were sacred creatures: the goat of Thor, the thunder god; and the golden-bristled pig of Frey, god of light and peace and of the earth's fruitfulness. Now they are simply a beloved part of Swedish Christmas. Straw symbolizes grain, therefore food and prosperity. That is why these animals as well as angels, tiny baskets, roosters, even Christmas stars are made of straw.

This grain symbol is used outdoors, too. Scandinavian families tie big bunches of grain to poles set up in their yards for the birds. Even people who live in apartments follow the old custom and tie bundles of grain to the corner posts of their balconies outside their windows.

All the time that these preparations are going on, people are buying or making Christmas gifts.

The cities' glittering department stores are filled with shoppers. And in brightly lit outdoor markets, especially set up for the season, crowds move among the gay old-fashioned booths in search of handmade Scandinavian treasures.

School is still in session, and the children are busy in the craft classes finishing up gifts for their families. At home, the grown-ups are also hurrying with knitting, sewing, carving, and hammering. Then everything is carefully hidden away until wrapping time.

A few days before Christmas, everyone is full of secrets. Behind closed doors can be heard the rustling of paper, and there is the pungent smell of hot sealing wax. Gifts are being wrapped, and each one is sealed carefully with a blob of melted wax. The very smell of hot sealing wax means Christmas to the Swedes all their lives.

The parcels, even when wrapped and sealed, are not yet ready. There are long silences between wrappings, and the curious listener knows that the person inside is deep in thought, composing Christmas verses. For each gift must be accompanied by a funny jingle which half-reveals, half-conceals what is in the package.

The Christmas Tree

A few days before Christmas, children are dismissed from school for a three-week holiday. Now at last the family can choose a Christmas tree. In the country people go out into the woods on foot or on skis, or drive off in a sleigh, or chain-equipped car, to select a fine straight hemlock or spruce. They also cut heaps of branches of fragrant juniper and pine to bring home for decorations. In the city, small forests of fresh spruce trees suddenly appear in the marketplaces. Families arrive at the market in groups so that every member can help make this important choice. The tree must be a *Julgran*, the most beautiful and the biggest tree the family can possibly afford.

Once it has been set up at home, the tree is decorated with only a few simple ornaments. The manger scene, perhaps carved by a great-grandfather, is arranged on a table nearby. The gifts, all the carefully hoarded and wrapped treasures, are put into a wicker basket on the floor. Large items, which cannot be wrapped, are covered by sheets or blankets to disguise their shapes. And now it is December 24, and the Christmas house is ready for the celebration.

Julafton (Christmas Eve)

This is the day everyone has been waiting for, the day of celebrating at home. At six o'clock all the members of the family gather in the spotless, fragrant kitchen for a special ceremony. Copper pots gleam, the kitchen is gay with paper garlands and holiday decorations. Candles glow in the three-branched candlestick which symbolizes the Trinity. The electric light is switched off, leaving only the six-pointed Star of Bethlehem shining in the window. There is a moment of quiet as the spirit of Christmas fills all hearts. Then mother moves toward the stove. There stands a kettle of steaming broth in which a ham, or perhaps a Christmas sausage called *korv*, has been boiled.

Each person spears a piece of dark brown bread with a fork, dips it into the kettle and eats. This time-honored ceremony of *doppa i grytan* (the dipping in the kettle) always comes before the real Yule feasting "for luck." It is in memory of a long ago time when the people were so poor that all they had for their Christmas feast was thin broth and black bread. Today the bread, *vörtbrod*, is brown and rich and sweet, and the broth is deliciously flavored.

After everyone has dipped his bread, it is time to begin the feast. Father says, *"God Yul! (Good Yule!)"* Wishes for happiness are exchanged. Perhaps there will be *glög*, a Swedish Christmas punch made of wine, raisins, dried figs, blanched almonds, and spices. Glög means "glow," and this punch gets its name from the burning of sugar cubes over the mixture before serving. Glasses filled with this heady beverage are lifted in toasts to the season. Then in a jolly mood the family sits down to dinner.

The meal begins with a splendid *smörgasbord*, appetizing spreads for bread. The traditional cod fish, the *lutfisk* or sun-cured cod, which took weeks to prepare, comes next. Fluffy and white, it is served with boiled potatoes, green peas, and a special white sauce. Then comes a rosy Christmas ham and a variety of breads.

No Christmas feast is complete without at least one serving of rice porridge, *risgrynsgröt*. The rice, cooked for hours in milk and sugar, thickens into a pudding which will be decorated on top with patterns of sifted cinnamon. Inside is hidden a single almond, or sometimes a small gold ring, so the dessert is eaten with care. If an unmarried person finds the almond or ring, that one is sure to be married during the coming year. When a child gets the lucky portion, there is much laughter and teasing and fun.

This is a large meal, and from the children's point of view, it is eaten much too slowly. At last it is over. Perhaps the grown-ups would like to take a nap, but no, the tree awaits!

Everyone moves into the living room. And there's the tree, and the basket overflowing with presents. This is the best time yet!

Father lights the white candles on the green tree branches. When the flickering wicks steady into a warm glow, the electric lights are turned off in the room, and everyone is very still. All eyes are fixed on the glowing tree. Someone quietly slips away from the family group.

A knock is heard upon the front door! *Rap, rap, rap!* The children gasp. This can only be *Jultomten,* the small, gnomelike creature who is the Swedish Santa Claus! The door is opened, and in he comes. Bowed under the sackful of presents, he tries to look small in the dim glow of candlelight. Disguising his voice as best he can, the father, uncle, or an elder brother plays the part of the beloved gnome. "Are there any good children in this house?"

he asks. Of course there are! All of them! And so the presents from the sack are given out to the young people. The little ones are too shy and awed by the Jultomten to say anything as they take their gifts. But their older brothers and sisters re-member to say, "*Tack.* (Thank you.)"

"God Jul! God Jul!" With a jerky little nod, Jultomten leaves "to go to the next house."

While the gifts are being opened and examined, the missing family member returns and looks sur-prised at all the activity.

"Oh, you have missed all the fun! Jultomten was here!" the young voices inform him with regret.

"Ah, but that is too bad," exclaims the one who played the part so successfully. "I shall be more careful next year, so I will not miss him."

The Swedish Santa is not jolly and noisy and fat. He is a skinny *tomte*, or little man, with a bit of a temper. For time beyond memory he has existed in rural Sweden as the guardian spirit of the farm. Each farm had its own tomte who lived in the hayloft and kept a sharp eye on everything. If he was well treated, things on the farm went well. But if the household tomte felt ill used, look out! Anyone with a grain of sense knew that if cows were to give milk, horses foal, crops grow in plenty, and the farm stay free of accidents, it was important to remember the tomte, especially on Christmas Eve. He liked porridge, so it was the custom to place a big bowl in the hayloft for him to enjoy after he had made his last round of the barns and stables. Even today this ceremony is observed in the country.

When it is possible, the family Jultomten arrives in a sleigh, but the sleigh is not drawn by reindeer. It is hitched to one or two goodnatured goats! And that is why the Swedish children love their Christmas goats.

After Jultomten leaves, there is still the basketful of presents to be given out to the family. There is the reading of the verses, the guessing of "what is it?" before paper is torn off and each gift is admired. By the time the last gift is fished out of the basket, it is quite late, and the family members bid each other good-night: "May God bless your Christmas; may it last till Easter."

Candles are blown out, and everyone goes to bed. The night's sleep will be sound but short. By four in the morning all must be up and stirring in order to get to church on time. Again candles glow in the windows "to light the Christ-child on his way," wake-up coffee and cocoa is served, and the family is off for the six o'clock service.

Christmas in the Country

In the central and northern parts of the country, where there is usually plenty of snow by this time, people still go to church in the old-fashioned way. They pile into sleighs big enough to hold eight besides the driver. Torches are lit and pushed into metal rings fastened to the outer sides of the sleighs. Rugs and furs are wrapped chin high to keep out the wind. With a shout from the driver, off goes the sleigh, bells jingling. The breath of the fat, snorting horses billows from their nostrils like steam in the cold air.

The forest looms dark and mysterious in the fitful light of the flaring torches. Strange, eerie shadows seem to leap out at the sleighs. The little ones tremble, and even the older boys and girls shiver.

"Listen!" a mother gives the children on either side of her a gentle shake. On the crisp winter air evergreens whisper and sigh. The frost-brittle branches of other trees snap like pop guns. "Look there!" mother points.

84

Now, from the side roads, come the cheerful glow of torches and the jingle of bells from other sleighs. Up the main road glides sleigh after sleigh, the runners *shush-shushing*, the bells jingling louder and louder, the pounding of the horses' hooves muffled by the snow. And there, in the distance, is the church, each window alight with candles.

Everyone hurries up the path, two by two, with flaming torches held high. As each worshiper draws near the building, he tosses his torch onto a crackling pile, which flares up into the darkness with a shower of sparks. Church doors open, and the organ music floats out into the dark morning. It is an old Lutheran hymn, "All Hail the Beauteous Morning Star." Before the altar is the shining radiance of hundreds of burning tapers.

> *Now light one thousand Christmas lights*
> *On dark earth here tonight*
> *One thousand, thousand also shine*
> *To make the dark sky bright.*

Congregation and choir raise their voices in joyous old hymns. Christ is born, and light will soon return to the earth. The old and the new customs have been observed. It is time to go home, to breakfast and a quiet day of rest.

Christmas visiting comes on *Annandagen*, the Day after Christmas, when the social life of the holiday begins. Then it is proper to make calls. And, if the family has not danced through the house before, they do it now, along with their visitors. The line grows as aunts, uncles, cousins, and friends join in, hand in hand, up and down, round and round, singing:

> *Oh now it's Christmastime*
> *And now it's Christmastime*
> *And Christmas lasts right up to Lent-time.*

10. THE NEW YEAR
IN SCANDINAVIA

New Year's in Denmark

New Year's Eve is mischief night for Danish young people. On every street small groups smother laughter as they creep up to ring neighbors' doorbells, change nameplates, or make off with a doormat someone forgot to take inside. A boy pushes a handful of dry beans through a mail slot, and runs away shouting as the beans skitter-clatter all over the floor inside. On the next block someone sets off a string of "jumping" firecrackers. Fireworks bang away, and smaller crackers hiss, sputter, and pop all through the evening.

In some areas, sometime during the fall, the

country children begin to collect cracked and broken crockery. Then, on New Year's Eve, they gather in excited groups and throw it against the house doors of their friends and neighbors. Years ago the noise and broken crockery were meant to be good-luck charms. The noise frightened off evil, and the broken shards of earthenware made it difficult for spirits to cross the threshold. The most popular family in the village had the biggest heap of broken crockery on the doorstep New Year's morning.

In villages where the custom is still followed, the master of each bombarded home must play his part. When the noise stops, he rushes out to catch the "good-luck throwers." They try to run away, but part of the fun is to be caught, because then they are brought into the house and treated to hot chocolate, cakes, cookies, and doughnuts.

Pranks and jokes are played on the farmers, too. Anything that isn't locked up safely in the barns is liable to be found in some unlikely place the next day. Garden gates swing from flagpoles; wheelbarrows somehow land on the rooftops of outbuildings; and ladders may be found in the wells. Of course it is all blamed on the "evil spirits" of old.

At midnight, in towns and cities, beautifully dressed people on the streets wish each other Happy New Year. Banquets, dances, dinners, and formal parties are part of the evening's entertainment. And in the homes, Christmas candles are lighted again, and there is laughter and good food.

New Year's in Norway

Young people in Norway often put on fancy costumes and masks and go visiting in groups of ten or more on New Year's Eve. They stop at every welcoming "open house" along the way for music, dancing, and refreshments. As one group drives away, another takes its place. Happily weary, each group finally winds up for breakfast at the home of some special friend.

Morning church services are the custom for January first. Afterward many people spend a quiet day at home, while others pay New Year's calls on friends and neighbors and then return home for dinner. The meal starts with a table full of cold appetizers, known as *koldt bord*. Strong holiday beer flows, and hearty good wishes are passed between host and guest as each bids the other luck and cheer for the coming year.

New Year's in Sweden

As midnight approaches, many Swedish families gather near the radio or television set for the special New Year's Eve programs. A favorite, which has been a tradition since the mid-1920s, is the reading of verses from Tennyson's *In Memoriam*, translated into Swedish. Old and young sit entranced by the splendid voice of a famous actor:

> *Ring out, wild bells...*
> *Ring out the old, ring in the new,*
> *Ring, happy bells, across the snow...*
> *Ring in the valiant man and free,*
> > *The larger heart, the kindlier hand;*
> > *Ring out the darkness of the land.*

Father pours a spicy, syrupy wine into small glass mugs and hands it around. On the stroke of twelve everyone drinks a toast to the New Year! Outside, factory and ship sirens shriek and hoot. People in the streets wish each other well. Here and there fireworks crack and shoot into the sky from apartment-house balconies.

And then, above all the wild noise and shouting, comes the peal of bells from the churches. As the more worldly noises cease, church bells all over the land peal out, deep and thrilling, melodious or wildly gay. One can imagine that the sound of the bells of all the churches in Sweden—in the whole of Scandinavia—join each other to ring in the New Year. What will the new year bring?

Saint Knut's Day

Yuletime celebrating goes right on to January thirteenth, Saint Knut's Day, when the season comes to an official close. King Canute, who ruled Denmark, England, and Norway a thousand years ago, decreed that Yule feasting should last 20 days, from Christmas Day to January 13. And since then, in Scandinavia, it always has.

"King Knut drives Christmas away," is an old Norwegian saying. And, as if to help him, country people once held races on this day. They piled into their sleighs and drove madly across the ice-covered lakes and frosty roads, with bells jingling and whoops and shouts ringing on the cold air.

In Sweden, this last day of the holiday is not allowed to slip quietly into things past. It calls for another party. Why? To dismantle the tree!

Party hats appear, music fills the house. If there is a musician available, that is best; if not, there

is always the record player. And of course there is singing. The tree is lighted for the last time, and the family gazes at it thoughtfully. Then it's *Julgransplundring!* (plunder time!) The little children "plunder" the cookies and candies from the branches and pop them into their mouths. Older ones take off the ornaments and pack them away in boxes. Small heart-shaped straw or paper baskets, filled with tiny goodies, are passed around. And finally, the bare tree is taken off its stand.

And *then* anyone walking past a Swedish house had better look sharp. Because the custom is to heave the tree out through the window! Even apartment-house dwellers sometimes get carried away, and *phweeuet*, before they've given it a second thought, out flies the tree! *Look out below!*

With the tree gone, and the window firmly shut by mother, everyone sings:

> *The twentieth day, King Knut did rule*
> *Would end the festival of Yule.*

The longest holiday season in Scandinavia is over. But as soon as people catch their breath they'll be off on the round of holiday celebrations all over again—in the New Year!

PRONOUNCING GUIDE

The accented syllable in each word is written in capital letters.

äggtoddy	EGG toddy
bunad	BOO nad
Dalarna	DAA lar na
Dannebrog	DAN ne bro
doppa i grytan	DOP pa ee GREE tan
ett å två å tre	ETT o TVO o TRREY
fettisdagsbulle	FEE yet tis dass booler
glög	GLUGG
Holmenkollen	HOL men KOL len
Jonsok	YON sok
Julafton	YULE AF ton
Julbockar	YULE BO kar
Julgran	YULE GRAAN
Julgrisar	YULE GREE sar
Julgransplundring	YULE GRAANS PLON dring
koldt bord	KOLT boer
Luciadagen	loo SEE a DAAG en
Lussekatter	LOO se KAAT ter
lutfisk	LUTE fisk
majstång	MY stong
Midsommar	MID sommar
pepparkakor	PEPPAR KAA kor
risgrynsgröt	REES greens GRUT
Rjukan	RHOO kan
Sankt Hans Aften	sank hans AF ten
Skartorsdag	SHARE tors daag
smörgasbord	SMER goes boord
terner	THAIR ner
Uppsala	OUP saa la
Valdemar	VAL de mar
Värmland	VAIRM land
vörtbrod	VORT brud

INDEX